Skateboard

KERRI MAZZARELLA

Table of Contents

A Pelican Book

Teaching Tips for Caregivers and Teachers:

Research shows that one of the best ways for students to learn a new topic is to read about it.

Before Reading

- Read the title and predict what the book will be about.
- Read the "Words to Know" and discuss the meaning of each word.
- Read the back cover to see what the book is about.

During Reading

- When a student gets to a word that is unknown, ask them to look at the rest of the sentence to find clues to help with the meaning of the unknown word.
- Motivate students with praise and encouragement.

After Reading

- Discuss the main idea of the book.
- Ask students to give one detail that they learned in the book.

SIGHT WORDS

a
and
at
for
fun
has
I
is
my
ride
the
this
use
with

Words to Know

friends

helmet

pads

park

skateboard

wheels

This is my **skateboard**.

My skateboard has **wheels.**

I use a **helmet** and **pads**.

I ride my skateboard at the **park**.

I ride my skateboard with **friends**.

I ride my skateboard for fun!

Written by: Kerri Mazzarella
Design by: Jen Bowers
Series Development: James Earley

Photos: Shutterstock.com/cover ©2022 kornnphoto, cover & interior sports icons ©Geanine87; p.3 & 13 ©2020 Dean Drobot; p.3 & 9 ©2022 Troyan; p.3 & 10, 11 ©2017 FamVeld ; p.3 & 5 ©2018 TheFarAwayKingdom; p.3 & 7©2020 Zayats Svetlana; p.4 ©2019 Max kegfire; p.6 ©2016 Grisha Bruev; p.8 ©2022 kornnphoto; p.12 ©2021 FamVeld; p.14 ©2022 Rido; p.15 ©2018 Ljupco Smokovski

Library of Congress PCN Data
Skateboard /Kerri Mazzarella
My 1st
ISBN 979-8-8873-5326-5 (hard cover)
ISBN 979-8-8873-5411-8 (paperback)
ISBN 979-8-8873-5496-5 (EPUB)
ISBN 979-8-8873-5581-8 (eBook)
Library of Congress Control Number: 2022948434
Printed in the United States of America.

Seahorse Publishing Company
www.seahorsepub.com

Published in the United States
Seahorse Publishing
PO Box 771325
Coral Springs, FL 33077